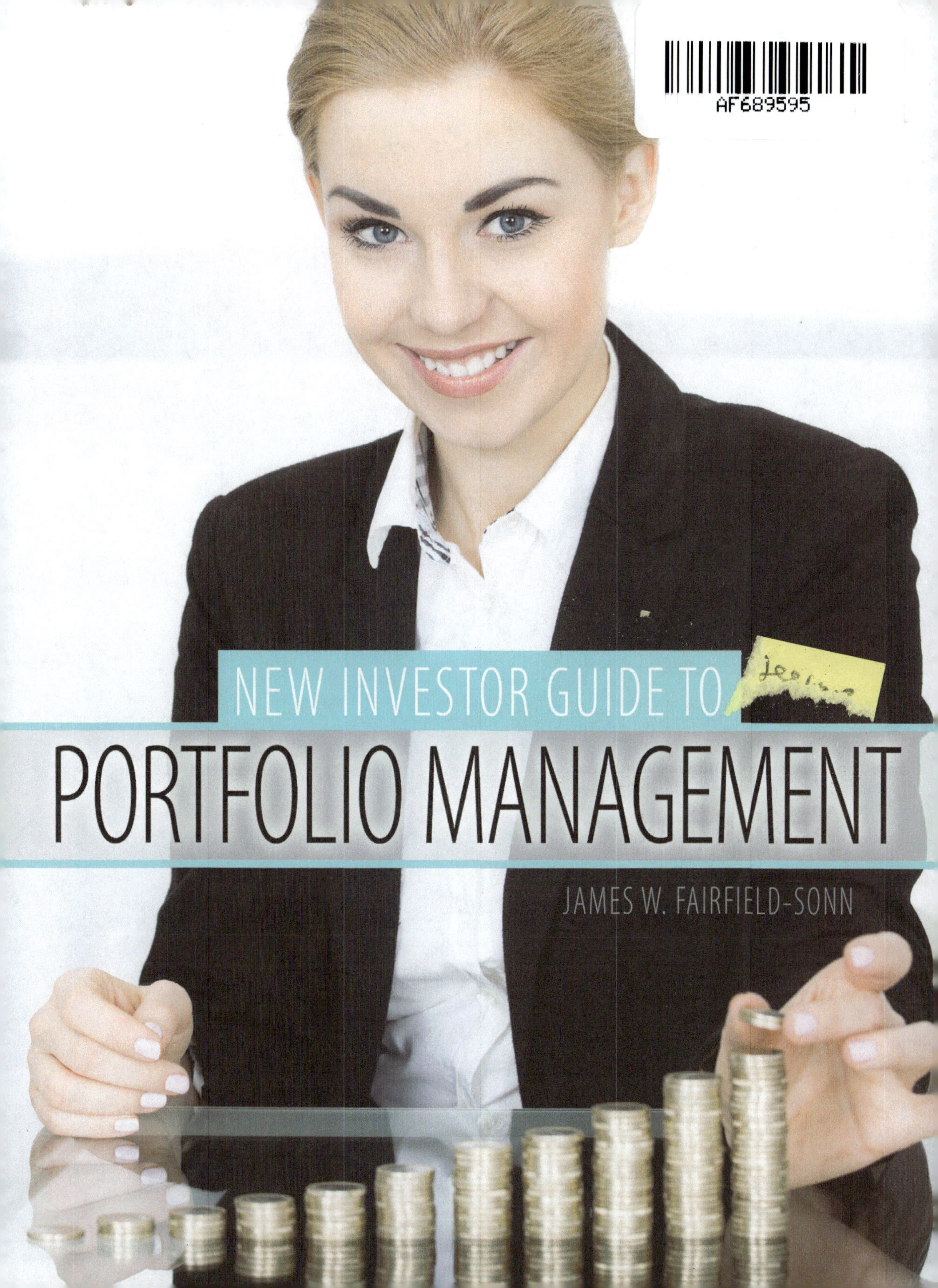

NEW INVESTOR GUIDE TO

PORTFOLIO MANAGEMENT

JAMES W. FAIRFIELD-SONN

Kendall Hunt
publishing company

www.kendallhunt.com
Send all inquiries to:
4050 Westmark Drive
Dubuque, IA 52004-1840

ISBN 978-1-4652-7169-3

Contents

PART 6

PART 7

New Investor Guide to Portfolio Management

PART 1

INTRODUCTION

While you may never have thought about yourself as an Investor as soon as you had any money available to use at your discretion you became one. The aim of this book is to help you think more clearly and carefully about how you use your money because your decisions will impact the quality of your life both now and in the future in so many ways.

As the title of this book suggests, the discussion here is aimed primarily at helping you to start and manage a collection of stocks, which in the investing world is called a ***portfolio***. Accordingly, the central focus here is on evaluating, buying, and selling stocks that are traded on open markets. The larger goal of this book is to provide you with a framework for understanding why having an investment portfolio should become an important part of a much larger approach to prudent investing that begins with establishing a realistic annual budget and leads to a flexible financial management plan that evolves over time in response to changing life conditions and needs.

IMPORTANCE OF INVESTING FOR THE FUTURE

Today's world of business is global, fast-paced, highly interconnected, and constantly changing. Despite the complexity of business, at the end of the day all business, including investing, comes down to a fundamental relationship between ***risk and reward***. Accordingly, whenever and wherever you invest your money, you are making a decision about how much risk you are willing to take in relation to the rewards that you hope to gain. In practice, this usually means that if the risk you are willing and able to bear is relatively low, then in all likelihood the expected rewards will also be relatively low. On the other hand, if you are open and capable of taking on more risk, then the potential rewards should be greater.

To aid you in becoming a more successful Investor, throughout this book, we will discuss how you can become more skilled at evaluating potential risks and rewards, in general, so you can make even more informed investment decisions over time. In addition, we will discuss how investment decisions need to be viewed not only from a short-term perspective, but also from a medium-term and long-term perspective because the risks and rewards associated with any particular investment will vary depending on how long you plan to make an investment in a stock or any other investment opportunity.

PART 2

GETTING STARTED

When is the best time to get started with your investment plans? Given the tremendous ***impact of time*** on the value of your investments, the best time to get started may be today! This is because, as we will discuss below, the amount of time you have to allow your investments to grow is far more important than the timing of when you make any specific investment. So, once you are clear on your general investment goals and comfortable with how much you can and will invest, then the time is right to start investing.

BASIC INVESTMENT ADVICE

As you start making your investment plans, you will soon discover that there is no shortage of specific advice on what to, when to, and where to invest your money. While any piece of specific advice will in all likelihood contain some elements of wisdom, in evaluating the usefulness of any specific piece of advice, the most important question to ask yourself is always, to what degree does this specific advice match my investment goals? In other words, while you should be open to considering any investment advice, the answer to the above question will let you know if the specific advice you are evaluating should be central, of moderate interest, or of only of passing interest to you and your investment decisions.

There are at least three pieces of basic advice that will be valuable to you in whatever investment decisions you make as part of a larger investment plan. First, as noted by Benjamin Franklin, "An investment in knowledge pays the best interest" (Franklin, 1758). In other words, if you want to be a successful Investor, you need to be prepared to commit time and effort to the study of how different types of investments work and do not work in the short term, medium term, and long term. Second, from investment guru Warren Buffett, know that armed with your ever growing knowledge of investing you always need to be both a Player and you should play for the long term (Cunningham, 2009). The reasoning behind this piece of basic advice is simple. If you are not actively involved in making investment decisions, then there will be no opportunity to benefit from them. Therefore, you should not let the fear of potential short-term losses or lack of experience in investing deter you from participating in the market over time. Indeed, it is only through experience that you can become a more successful Investor and in the long run you can learn as much from investments that work out poorly as those that work out well. Third, from Peter Lynch, one of the foremost Investment Advisors, invest in things you know (Lynch, 1996). In other words, if you are familiar with a particular product, service, company, industry, or market segment it is more likely that you can accurately predict how well stocks in that area will perform, which will, in turn, increase the probability that you will be able to identify when to buy or sell any particular stock(s).

BASIC INVESTMENT CONCEPTS

As you start investing, there are some basic concepts that will help you become more successful. Some of the most important basic concepts are briefly discussed as follows.

Putting Money to Work

You work hard for your money. Once you have money, you have four basic choices to make. One choice is to immediately spend all your money to buy things or services that you want or need today. Another choice is to put your money aside to be used at some time in the future. The third choice is to invest your money for the future in the hope of making more money on that investment and that additional money will, in turn, lead you to make even more money in the future. The fourth choice is to allocate your money in some combination of the three choices listed above.

Your decision about how to use your money, therefore, comes down to a choice about how much money you will spend today versus how much you will hold aside for another day and/or invest for the future? In practice, if you decide to spend all your money today, you can have some immediate satisfaction, but your future becomes more uncertain. If you decide to let your money set aside, you will forego some immediate satisfaction and your future may be less uncertain than if you had spent the money because you now have resources that can be used in many ways at a later point in time. Following this path does, however, have a potential risk that you also need to consider. Namely, for many reasons you need to know that a dollar today does not always have the same purchasing power as a dollar tomorrow. This is because of the potential influence of what is called ***inflation*** or ***deflation*** on the value of that dollar at some point in the future. Specifically, a dollar today can lose purchasing power if the cost of goods and services that can be bought with that dollar increases over time, we call this inflation. On the other hand, if the cost of goods and services that can be bought with that dollar decreases over time, we call this deflation. The third option is to put your money to work through some type of investment. This choice means that you will pass on some immediate satisfaction in the hope of eventually having even more money over time to purchase things that are important for you to have at some time in the future.

How any individual Investor will determine the best way to put their money to work today is a personal matter that reflects both current conditions and their future plans. Choices have consequences and so it is best to make choices that take into consideration your short-, medium-, and long-term goals.

The Impact of Time and Rate of Return on an Investment—Rule of 72

For that portion of your money that you decide to invest, an important and useful general question to ask is, how long will it take for my money to double in value? This relationship is called compounding and it is well known by most seasoned Investors.

Fortunately, there is a fairly simple way to make this determination that is called the Rule of 72. The Rule of 72 works in the following way. If you know how much your investment will increase in value over time, for example, 9% a year, then, by dividing this number into 72 tells you that it will take about eight years to double. On the other hand, if you want to double your money in five years then dividing 5 into 72 tells you that the interest rate you will need to reach this goal is 14.4%. This Rule is very helpful because it clearly shows the relationship between any given rate of return and the amount of time it will take to double your investment, which, in turn, can be very useful to you with your overall investment planning. Specifically, by understanding the power of compounding it becomes easier to plan what rewards may come from any short-term (e.g., days to months); a medium-term (e.g., three to five years); or a long-term (e.g., over five year) investment and this can become a great tool in developing your overall financial plan.

Why Starting to Invest Early Is a Good Thing

With the above discussion by way of background, it becomes easier to see why the earlier you can start investing the greater the likelihood that you will be able to enjoy the benefits of investing. So, you should think about making some type of investment(s) as soon as you can in order to increase the likelihood of realizing your investment goals.

To illustrate the above point not only for early, but also consistent investing consider the four following situations where an Investor is not just making a one-time investment, but is also committed to making the same level of investment year-over-year to reach a long-term goal, in this case retirement.

Investor 1 commits to investing US$2500 a year at age 35 until he is 65 with the hope of having an annual 5% return. This will yield a retirement nest egg of roughly US$174,000.

Investor 2 commits to investing US$2500 a year at age 35 until she is 65 with the hope of having an annual 10% return, which is a little less than the average annual stock market return for the last 75 years. This will yield a retirement nest egg of roughly US$452,000.

While the above returns look good, consider what happens to Investors who start at age 25 as opposed to age 35.

Investor 3 commits to investing US$2500 a year at age 25 until she is 65 with the hope of having an annual 5% return. This will yield a retirement nest egg of roughly US$317,000.

Investor 4 commits to investing US$2500 a year at age 25 until he is 65 with the hope of having an annual 10% return. This will yield a retirement nest egg of roughly US$1,217,000.

Maximize Rewards and Minimize Risk Through Diversification

Given the importance of yields to investing results, we need to note here that as discussed in the Introduction to this Guide, all business transactions come down to the fundamental relationship between ***risk and reward***. With that important point in mind, you should know that one of the best ways to maximize rewards and minimize risks in a stock portfolio over time is to diversify your holdings. That is to say, if you only purchase one stock you have great potential for reward, but, at the same time, you are facing a great risk. So, to increase the likelihood of long-term rewards while also minimizing the downside risk of any one investment turning out badly, it is wise to invest in a number of different stocks, perhaps for a variety of different reasons, that you believe will do well in the future.

Market Timing Versus Dollar Cost Averaging

The above discussion makes a strong case for why an Investor should always be a Player. As a practical matter the question remains, when should an Investor buy and sell stocks? Ideally, every Investor would like to buy stocks when they are low and sell them when they are high. However, the reality is that the stock market, in general, and individual stocks, in particular, often move in somewhat unpredictable ways for reasons that are not always transparent or understandable. So, what should a prudent Investor do to maximize their rewards while minimizing risks?

Here, there are three basic choices. One choice is to try to time the market such that investments are made when individual stocks are undervalued and sell them when they seem to be overpriced. Another option is to look beyond the swings in the market and consistently buy stocks that are seen as having long-term value and selling stocks that do not. The third possibility is to combine both approaches over time as conditions change. Below are two more discussions about basic investing concepts related to buying and selling stocks that may likewise prove to be helpful.

Do Not Fall in Love With Your Investments

After researching an investment and deciding why it is a good investment in the short term, medium term, or long term, it is important that you do not assume that everything will turn out exactly as you planned. Any number of things can happen within an organization and/or in the external market that can alter, sometimes dramatically, the future prospects for a company and its stock value. So, it is best to become a Disciplined Investor and periodically monitor the performance of the company and news about recent developments that may impact the company, in general. In addition, it is advisable to set performance goals that may "trigger" an action on your part. For example, you might set a trigger for when your investment declines by 10% to evaluate whether or not it would be wise to sell all the stock as a way to minimize future risks. You might also set a trigger for when the investment increases by 10% so that you will perhaps need to consider selling half of the stock. In the same vein, you might have made an investment with the hope that the value of the stock would increase by 20% in a year. Much to your pleasant surprise, the stock increases by 20% in six months! This is wonderful news, but at this time you should not fall in love with your stock and assume it will continue to increase in value at the same rate forever. Rather, this would be a great time to (re)evaluate the stock and its prospects for the future. This analysis, could lead to any number of different decisions ranging from: it is time to sell some more of the stock; it is time to sell all of the stock; or it is time to buy more of the stock.

The Past Is Not Always the Best Predictor of the Future

Finally, along with not falling in love with a stock, you also need to be aware that past performance is not always the best predictor of the future (Gladwell, 2002). Many Investors buy a stock based on past performance that indicates a steady increase in value. While this approach to selecting stocks seems reasonable on the surface, it is even more important to understand the reasons that led the stock to increase in value in the first place and then to ask yourself if those conditions are still in place? If the conditions are still in operation, then it may make sense to buy the stock. On the other hand, what you may find is that after a stock has increased in value for some time, for a variety of reasons, other Investors are concluding that the stock has reached a peak and therefore they are less interested in making future investments in the stock because they think it has reached a high and they are now selling the stock. Likewise, you should not rule out investing in a stock that has been declining. There are many reasons for a stock to lose value and many Investors are actually very interested in these stocks because they hope to be able to buy the stock at a low price and benefit from its rebound.

PART 3

MANAGING YOUR INVESTMENTS

Given the above basic investment advice and the discussion of several basic investment concepts, you now can see why actively managing your investments is strongly advised for anyone who is involved in buying and selling stocks. At a minimum, good management consists of three interrelated activities: setting investment goals; tracking your investments; and learning from your investment experience. Each of these important points is discussed as follows.

Setting Investment Goals

There is a great deal of research that indicates "Setting Goals" leads to better results than "Doing Your Best." This is true in virtually every endeavor from engaging in a healthier life style to making moves aimed at advancing your career to managing your investments. So, as you start to think about effectively managing your investments, the best place to start is by establishing some goals that you want to pursue. Specifically, you should begin by identifying somewhere between three to-five goals to guide your investment efforts. In deciding on what goals to pursue, you should know that there are no universal "Best" goals; rather the best goals are those that reflect where you are in your current life and where you want to be at some point in the future. By the way, when thinking about setting goals, you should never limit yourself to only one goal, because we also know from research that the single-minded pursuit of just one goal typically leads to negative long-term results.

What kind of investment goals should you consider? The best general guidance here is to pursue a combination of goals that collectively will maximize your rewards while minimizing your risks. More precisely, when it comes to setting investing goals having some definite financial goals is clearly important, but there are other goals that can also be equally important over the long run to an Investor and so they should likewise be given serious consideration. For example, setting a financial goal of making a profit, in general, is a good place to start. However, setting a more specific target (e.g., 5%) within a specific timeframe (e.g., six months) is even better. At the same time, giving thought to ways to minimize risks is equally important. So, you might also want to consider including a goal(s) aimed at minimizing potential losses (e.g., diversifying your investments). Some examples of financial goals that you might want to consider are discussed as follows.

- Increase the value of my portfolio by 10% during the next year.
- Diversify my portfolio by including at least five stocks.

- Invest in some companies that have established track records of growth.
- Make an investment in one company in a new rapidly growing market.
- Invest in a company with strong seasonal sales.

Given the importance of investing for the long term, there are also a number of other more general goals that are likewise worth considering as they will make you a more informed Investor over time and they can help you to more clearly define the composition of your portfolio. Some examples of these goals are listed as follows.

- Learn more effective ways to research a company's future prospects.
- Learn more about how stock markets behave over time.
- Develop a disciplined approach to following media news on firms.
- Follow firms whose products and/or services I know and use.
- Invest in companies whose products and/or services support ethical ends.

If you have not already set some investment goals, this would be a good time to begin. Start by identifying three to five goals that are of interest to you at this time, realizing that they can and probably will change over time.

My Investment Goals

Goal 1: ______________________________

Goal 2: ______________________________

Goal 3: ______________________________

Goal 4: ______________________________

Goal 5: ______________________________

Tracking Your Investments

After establishing your investment goals for a set period, the next step in disciplined investing is to create a way to record of your investment decisions over time. A very basic system is shown below that consists of: recording the name of the stock that is being traded; the quantity of stock that was bought or sold; on a particular date; at a given price; the potential buy and sell triggers to monitor; and the reason for the investment or the sale. This record can be set up on an excel spreadsheet or you may wish to use a commercially available recording system.

My Investment Record

Stock	#Bought/Sold	Date	Price	Triggers	Reason for Investment/Sale

Learning From Your Experience

If you have previous investing experience you can review your prior investment goals and the history of your past investments to discover what transactions went very well, those that went fairly well, and those that did not go well at all. Working with this information, you can begin to refine your investment strategy to improve on your results given your future investment plans.

If you have never bought or sold a stock before, you might want to become more familiar with investing, in general, by first creating a "Paper" portfolio to learn more about the process. One easy, yet effective way to do this is to begin by assuming that you have US$100,000 in cash to invest over the next three months, knowing that you have a set amount of money to invest, next establish some investment goals. With your goals in mind, identify five to ten companies that are of potential interest to you as investments. Over the next three months, as you find good reasons to buy or sell these stocks, do so, recording the reason(s) for each transaction in your investment record. Based on the information developed from the paper portfolio exercise, you will now have some useful information that you can review and analyze as you prepare to make your first investment.

PART 4

RECOGNIZING STOCK MARKET INVESTMENT OPPORTUNITIES

The decision about when it would be a good time to buy or sell any particular stock involves many considerations. At a minimum, it is important to simultaneously consider four things that are discussed below in coming to your final decision. These considerations are: overall stock market trends; specific market segment trends; individual company conditions; and your investment horizon.

Learning About Stock Market Trends

An important part of learning more about stock market opportunities is to become aware of how the stock market has behaved in the past, is currently behaving, and what is likely to happen in the future. As you research the history of the stock market, you will soon discover some of the reasons why over time: there have been periods of great growth in stock values, which are often referred to as "bull" markets; times when the value of stocks have declined significantly, which are usually called "bear" markets; and other times when the market seemed to be basically holding steady. Knowing this history can be valuable to you particularly when you examine how the market has been performing over the last few years, where it has been going most recently, and where it is likely to move in the future.

Fortunately, it is possible to learn a great deal about the past and current stock market conditions by reviewing the history of a number of established indicators of stock market performance. Three very good, but difference indicators that you should consider examining are the Dow Jones Industrial Average (DJIA), the Standard and Poor's 500 (S&P 500), and the Wilshire 5000. Each of these stock market indicators are briefly described as follows.

Dow Jones Industrial Average

One of the most closely watched indicators of stock market activity is called the DJIA. This "average" or index, first published in 1896, is useful to Investors because it shows how 30 major, United States-based, publically owned, companies traded during a standard trading session in the stock market. Given the size and diversity of the firms in this index, which include firms, such as 3M, General Electric, and Microsoft, it is considered to be a good indicator of how general economic and political developments around the world may influence the future performance of stocks not only in the index, but other stocks as well (Investopedia, 2015a).

Standard and Poor's 500

This stock market index, first published in 1957, is also closely watched by Investors because it consists of 500 large capitalization stocks that are traded on either the New York Stock Exchange (NYSE) or National Association of Securities Dealers Automated Quotations (NASDAQ). Given that this index includes a diverse set of growth and value stocks and the index is weighted based on the size of a stock's capitalization, liquidity, industry grouping and other factors, it provides a very good representation of the U.S. stock market, in general, and is considered by many to be a "bellweather" indicator of future developments in the American economy (Investopedia, 2015d).

Wilshire 5000 (TMWX)

If an Investor wants to know how most of the publically traded stocks on the NYSE, NASDAQ, and the American Stock Exchange are faring; the best source to turn to is the Wilshire 5000. This market-weighted capitalization index, first published in 1974, when there were approximately 5000 companies in this category. Today, it is currently composed of more than 6700 companies that are: headquartered in the United States; actively traded on an American stock exchange; and that have pricing information widely available to the public (Investopedia, 2015e).

UNDERSTANDING MARKET SEGMENT TRENDS

Within the general stock market, there are specific market segments that behave differently given changes in economic conditions. While there are many ways to describe these industry investment segments some commonly used classifications include: basic materials (steel and iron); consumer goods (appliances); financial (property and casualty insurance); healthcare (biotechnology); industrial goods (cement); service (home furnishing stores); technology (personal computers); and utilities (electric utilities). Looking into market segments to learn about trends is important to the identification of potential stock opportunities because different industries become more or less attractive given changes in the economy. For example, when the economy gets stronger more consumer goods can and usually are purchased. So, all things being equal, the values of stocks in this sector will likely increase in the short term.

FINDING INFORMATION ABOUT INDIVIDUAL COMPANIES

With an understanding of current stock market performance trends as well as segment trends, in mind, it is now easier to evaluate specific stocks that may be of interest as a potential investment. To do so, fortunately, there are many good open sources of information available to learn more about specific companies. Several of the best sources are: Finance.yahoo.com; the Wall Street Journal.com; and Bloomberg.com. By exploring these sites, it is possible to gather a great deal of valuable information about specific stocks.

Some of the most important information you will want to examine and evaluate includes; the company's earnings per share; capitalization; beta, which measures the volatility of the stock compared with the general market; and information about whether or not the stock pays a dividend and how large and frequently that dividend has been given.

MATCHING STOCKS TO YOUR INVESTMENT GOALS

Armed with information about overall stock market trends, specific market segment trend; and individual company reports; you are now in a good position to evaluate how wise it would be to buy or sell as stock at this time given your investment goals. The examples below illustrate some of the situations that you might encounter in deciding whether or not to buy or sell a "technology" stock (e.g., Apple, Microsoft) at a given point in time.

Situation 1: The overall stock market has been holding steady for the last several years. The technology segment has been increasing slightly for the last few months. The technology stock you are evaluating has just announced an exciting new product that they will be introducing to the market at the end of the month. Your interest, at this time, is to purchase a stock that might be able to appreciate significantly during the next six months.

While there are different ways to evaluate the above situation, many Investors might see this as a good investment opportunity given that while the overall market and the technology segment seems to be relatively stable, the company's new product launch could lead to a significant growth in revenue that could make the stock more attractive in the near term. So, the decision to buy some of this stock would make sense.

Situation 2: The overall stock market has been increasing steadily for the last several years. The technology segment has been holding steady for the last few months.

The technology stock you are evaluating has just announced that due to some problems in their supply chain management system, they have not been able to meet promised delivery commitments on many of their core products. Your interest, at this time, is to purchase a stock that might be able to appreciate somewhat during the next year.

As with Situation 1, there are many ways to evaluate the above situation. Many Investors might see this as a good time to sell this stock. The reason for this decision is based on a number of considerations. Specifically, while the overall market is doing well, which is a good thing, on the other hand, the technology sector has not been a key driver in this pattern of growth, so this would be a major concern. Perhaps more importantly, you believe that fixing problems with supply chain management systems for core products will probably not be easy for the company to address in the near term. If this assumption proves to be true, then in all likelihood revenues for the company will be decreasing for the foreseeable future, which will make the stock less attractive during the next year. So, the decision to sell some or all of this stock makes sense.

PART 5

PREPARING TO INVEST

Preparing to make an investment is an important decision that needs to be guided by at least three major considerations. First, you need to know how much you ***can*** invest at any point in time. Second, you need to be comfortable with how much you ***will*** invest. Third, you need to have a good sense of your ***investment objectives*** about when and how you intend to use the money that will hopefully result from your investment. Each of these considerations is briefly discussed as follows.

How Much CAN You Risk

To decide how much you can invest at any given time, it is important to first develop a ***personal budget*** that includes at least four basic considerations. These considerations are: how much annual income you will be receiving after deductions have been made for required taxes; your current fixed expenses; an estimate of how much money you want to commit to variable expenses; and the amount of money you want to set aside in a rainy day fund for emergencies. After taking these considerations into account, what remains will be the amount that you can realistically invest in any number of different ways.

Below is an illustration of how this system can work for you. Assume that you are living in Boston and have a job that pays US$48,000 a year after required taxes. In this case, your personal budget might look something like the one below.

My Personal Budget

Monthly Income	4000
Monthly Fixed Expenses	
Rent	1400
Utilities	200
Insurance	200
Monthly Variable Expenses	
Food	800
Transportation	400
Telephone	200
Entertainment	600
Monthly Saving for Emergencies	200
Monthly Contribution to a Fund for Investing	200

In the sample personal budget above you can see that US$200 month or US$2400 a year is the amount that can be invested. Given this information, the next question to be answered is how much will you invest and in what ways will you invest this money?

How Much WILL You Risk

The decision about how much you will invest and in what ways will you invest comes down to two basic considerations. These considerations are your tolerance for risk and your investment objectives. While there are many ways to describe an Investor's tolerance for risk, one easy way to start thinking about this is to ask if your tolerance for risk is low, moderate, or high?

As a practical matter, if your tolerance for risk is low, you would prefer an investment(s) that is quite safe even if the potential reward is low. On the other hand, if you have a moderate tolerance for risk, you might be more comfortable with a combination of investments that include some rather safe and risky investments. Alternatively, for Investors with a high tolerance for risk, their portfolio could reasonably consist primarily of potentially high risk and high reward investments. Clearly, knowing your tolerance for risk is important, but your final investment decisions will also need to take into account your investment goals as discussed in the following.

Begin With the End in Mind

While it is always exciting to get started on a new venture, it is equally important to also know at the outset where you hope the venture will take you and when it will end Along with knowing how much you can invest as well as your tolerance for risk, as you prepare to invest, it is equally important that you have a clear sense of your investment objectives. In other words, it is always important to begin with an end in mind. This is certainly true for investing. For example, if you are starting to invest as a way to learn more about how the stock market works, in general, and you are committed to doing so for one year, then this will help you to decide on what stocks you would most likely invest in during this time frame. On the other hand, if you are investing today, so you will be able to have enough money for a down payment on a house in 10 years, then you might well be interested in a somewhat different set of investments. Alternatively, if you are investing to create a retirement fund to live on in 30 years, then you might be more interested in yet another set of investment possibilities.

Whatever your investment goal(s) and investing horizon(s) are the important thing to remember is that you do not ever want to be forced to sell your stocks or bonds before you are ready to given your plans, in general. In particular, you do want to have to sell your stocks or bonds when they and the market as-a-whole are down. The best way to assure that this never happens to you, as discussed above, is by doing a very good job of realistically understanding what you can invest, will invest, and how long you plan to make the investment.

PART 6

MAKING AN INVESTMENT

After going through the exercises described above, you should now be in a good position to start using the funds you have identified as those for investing to start making more informed investment allocations within your portfolio. Initially, your funds will probably be primarily in the form of cash and you may want to always keep some of your funds in cash because it is the most liquid form of investment, but you can also now start to diversify your portfolio by buying some company stocks or bonds or other investments that you find to be interesting.

Investing in a Company

If your research has led you to the conclusion that you would like to invest in a company, there are three ways that you can do so and the decision reflects the fundamental relationship between risk and reward. The greatest risk and potential rewards come from buying "common" stock in a firm. A slightly less risky approach, but one that generally will be less rewarding, is to buy a "preferred" stock. The least risky way to invest in a company is to buy their bonds, but the yield or reward here is generally the lowest. The reasons for these differences in risk and reward are easy to understand. When there is money available to pay Investors, the Bond Holders get paid first, the Preferred Shareholders second, and the Common Stock holders last. Given the order and amount of dividends Investors are likely to receive, the underlying value of a Bond is most stable, followed by Preferred Stock holders, with the greatest volatility in value, up-and-down, will be with the Common Stock holders.

WHERE STOCKS AND BONDS ARE TRADED

Once you decide to buy a stock or bond, you can do so either through a broker or an online service. However, you decide to make your transaction, it will then go through an exchange or off-exchange market. Indeed, there are many exchange markets, throughout the world where stocks and bonds can be bought and sold. Below is a brief discussion of the top 10 exchanges throughout the world, listed by size, where many trades are made (World Stock Exchanges, 2015) as well as a description of the over-the-counter market.

1. New York Stock Exchange: The NYSE, sometimes also known as the "Big Board," was founded in 1817. Located in New York City, it is by far the largest stock trading exchange in the world with a market capitalization of approximately US$25 trillion U.S. dollars for the roughly 1800 companies that are listed there.

2. National Association of Securities Dealers Automated Quotations: NASDAQ was founded in 1971 as the world's first electronic stock exchange and is currently the second-largest exchange in the United States by market capitalization and trading volume (Investopedia, 2015c). Many of the largest technology and biotech firms such as Apple and Amgen are traded on this exchange. To be traded on this market, a small-, mid- or large-cap company must: be registered with the U.S. Security and Exchange Commission (SEC); have at least three market makers; and meet minimum asset, capital, public shares, and shareholders criteria (Investopedia, 2015b).
3. Tokyo Stock Exchange: Companies trading on this exchange are separated into three groups: first section for large companies; second section for mid-sized companies; and mothers section for high-growth startup companies.
4. London Stock Exchange: Founded in 1801, it is the oldest and most international of all the stock exchanges.
5. Shanghai Stock Exchange: This is one of only two stock exchanges in the People's Republic of China that operate independently. Unlike the Hong Kong Stock Exchange, it is not entirely open to foreign investors.
6. Hong Kong Stock Exchange: This exchange is the third largest in Asia and operates independently of the People's Republic of China.
7. Toronto Stock Exchange: This is the largest exchange in Canada and the third largest in North America. Several major mining as well as oil and gas companies are listed on this exchange.
8. BM&F Bovespa: Headquartered in Sao Paulo, Brazil, this is the largest exchange in South America.
9. Australian Securities Exchange: Formed in 2006 with the merger of the Australian Stock Exchange and the Sydney Futures Exchange, it is currently the primary securities exchange in Australia.
10. Deutsche Borse: Headquartered in Frankfurt, Germany, it provides many companies with access to global capital markets.

Over-the-counter or off-exchange transactions are not regulated by an exchange; rather they are done directly by two parties. In 2014, approximately 40% of the stock exchanges were done in this way. A concern with this so-called "Fourth Market" is that prices are often unpublished and unregulated (Wikipedia, 2015).

OTHER INVESTMENTS

While this book is primarily about investing in individual company stocks and bonds, as you become as more seasoned Investor there are many other forms of investment that you might also want to consider. Some of the more popular investments include index funds; precious metals, such as gold and silver; art; diamonds; and real estate.

PART 7

CONCLUDING THOUGHTS

Prudent investing is not about getting rich quick, but if you invest wisely, the likelihood that you will be able to have many things that you would like to have during your working years and into retirement will increase significantly.

What does it mean to invest wisely? As we discussed above, the first thing to remember is that given the power of compounding, the earlier you start investing the greater the chance will be that your investments will increase substantially in value. Second, being very clear about how much you can and will invest is critical because this will allow you to decide when to make or sell an investment, rather than ever being in a situation where you are forced to sell an investment before according to your plans the time is right. In this way, you can always be a Player. Third, as in so many areas of life, the probability of being a successful Investor increases when: you are clear about your investment goals; you are committed to always learning more about the process of investing, in general, as well as the risks and rewards of any given investment, in particular; and, you develop a disciplined approach to actively managing your investments.

Best wishes to you in all your investment decisions.

REFERENCES

Cunningham, L.A. (2009). *The essays of Warren Buffett: Lessons for investors and managers* (3rd ed.). Hoboken, NJ: John Wiley & Sons, 2009.

Franklin, B. (1758). *The way to wealth: Benjamin Franklin on money and success*. Carlisle, MA: Applewood Books.

Gladwell, M. (2002). *The tipping point: How little things can make a big difference*. New York, NY: Little, Brown and Company, 2002.

Investopedia. (2015a). *Dow jones industrial average—DJIA*. Retrieved from http://www.investopedia.com/terms/d/djia.asp

Investopedia. (2015b). *Nasdaq*. Retrieved from http://www.investopedia.com/terms/n/nasdaq.asp

Investopedia. (2015c). *Electronic trading: Nasdaq versus NYSE*. Retrieved from http://www.investopedia.com/university/electronictrading/trading1.asp

Investopedia. (2015d). *Standard & Poor's 500 Index—S&P 500*. Retrieved from http://www.investopedia.com/terms/s/sp500.asp

Investopedia. (2015e). *Wilshire 5000 Total Market Index*. Retrieved from http://www.investopedia.com/terms/w/wilshire5000equityindex.asp

Lynch, P. (1996). *Learn to earn: A beginner's guide to the basics of investing and business.* New York, NY: Simon & Schuster.

Wikipedia (2015). *Over-the-counter (finance).* Retrieved from http://en.wikipedia.org/wiki/Over-the-counter_(finance)

World Stock Exchanges. (2015). *Top 10 stock exchanges in the world.* Retrieved from http://www.world-stock-exchanges.net/top10.html

More Ideas on Investing

Malkiel, B.G. (2012). *A random walk down wall street: The time-tested strategy for successful investing.* (10th ed.). New York, NY: W.W. Norton & Co.

Malkeil, B.G.& Ellis, C.D. (2013) *The elements of investing: Easy lessons for every investor.* Hoboken, NJ: John Wiley & Sons, Inc.

Schroeder, A. (2009). *The Snowball: Warren Buffett and the business of life.* New York, NY: Bantam Books.

Siegel, J.J. (2002) *Stocks for the long run: The definitive guide to financial market returns and long-term investment strategies.* (3rd ed.). New York, NY: McGraw-Hill.

Useful Investment Blogs

To learn more investing ideas, it is recommended that you follow some well-known investment blogs. Below is a list of some blogs that you might find to be useful.

Get Rich Slowly. www.getrichslowly.org
Girls Just Want to have Funds
Learnvest
MoneyNing
Nerd Wallet
The Dough Roller
The Simple Dollar

Glossary of Investment Terms and Concepts

Diversification. To maximize rewards while minimizing risks in the long term, it is best to invest in a number of different stocks that have different potential reward and risk characteristics.

Impact of time on investment values. The most important variable in determining the potential future value of an investment is how much time you can hold the investment.

Inflation/Deflation. The cost of goods and services can increase over time due to economic and/or political forces at work in the world. When this happens, we call this inflation. The primary economic reasons for prices to increase are that demand is increasing and/or supply is decreasing. The primary political reasons for prices to rise are the decision by governments to increase the money supply or to lower taxes so individuals have more money to spend.

The cost of goods and services can also decrease over time due to economic and/or political forces at work in the world. When this happens, we call this deflation. The primary economic reasons for prices to decrease are that demand is decreasing and/or supply is increasing. The primary political reasons for prices to rise are the decision by governments to decrease the money supply or to raise taxes so individuals have less money to spend.

Investing in a company. You can invest in a company in three ways. The greatest risks and rewards are associated with buying common stocks. Moderate risks and rewards come with the purchase of preferred stock. The least risk and reward come from buying a bond.

Portfolio. A collection of financial assets, such as stocks, bonds, and cash, that are held and managed by an individual(s) or financial professionals and institutions according to an Investor's risk tolerance, investment time horizon, and investment objectives.

Risk and reward. All business, including investing, comes down to a fundamental relationship between risk and reward. Accordingly, whenever and wherever you invest your money, you are making a decision about how much risk you are willing to take in relation to the rewards that you hope to gain. In practice, this usually means that if the risk you are willing and able to bear is relatively low, then in all likelihood the expected rewards will also be relatively low. On the other hand, if you are open and capable of taking on more risk, then the potential rewards should be greater.

Biography

James W. Fairfield-Sonn received his BS degree from the University of Massachusetts (Amherst), MS degree from Cornell's School of Industrial and Labor Relations, and PhD degree from Yale. Currently, he is a tenured Professor of Management at the Barney School of Business within the University of Hartford. At the business school, he teaches courses in international business, leadership, and managerial skills. At this internationally accredited AACSB Business School, he was Chair of the Management Department from 1987 to 1990, Director of the Executive MBA Program from 1993 to 1995, Interim Dean from 2004 to 2005, and Dean from 2005 to 2013. In 1999, he won the first "Outstanding Teacher of the Year" Award at the Barney School of Business and in 2011 he was awarded a Fulbright Fellowship to Germany. He is also listed in Who's Who in America and Who's Who in the World. His research interests center primarily on understanding how corporate culture and quality practices influence organizational performance. In addition to lecturing throughout the United States and Europe on these topics, he has also published his findings in many journals and authored a book on the subject entitled, *Corporate Culture and the Quality Organization*. He has consulted with firms in the fields of architecture, chemicals, computers, defense, education, engineering, finance, health care, insurance, law, restaurants, and utilities. He is also a Member of the Old Lyme Congregational Investment Committee and the MacCurdy-Salisbury Educational Foundation.

Acknowledgments

The author wishes to acknowledge the contributions of many individuals who helped with the development of this book. First, all credit for making the design of the book more appealing goes to Anne Fairfield-Sonn who has a wonderful sense of style. Second, thanks goes to Jimmy Fairfield-Sonn for his careful reading of the work in progress and his thoughtful comments on ways that the content could be improved. In addition, a note of appreciation is in order for all the Students in the Barney School of Business BAR 110 World of Business course whose investment questions provided the framework for the organization of the book. Finally, sincere thanks to Dr Malek Lashgari, Professor of Finance and Dr Lillian Kamal, Associate Professor of Economics at the Barney School of Business for their support and interest in the development of this book.

Acknowledgments